Carl Robert Zache

Hero and Leander

A Poem

Carl Robert Zache

Hero and Leander
A Poem

ISBN/EAN: 9783337195236

Printed in Europe, USA, Canada, Australia, Japan

Cover: Foto ©Thomas Meinert / pixelio.de

More available books at **www.hansebooks.com**

A POEM

BY

CARL ROBERT ZACHE

NEW YORK

PUBLISHED BY THE AUTHOR

1884

Press of
G. P. Putnam's Sons
New York

TO

STEPHEN BULL, ESQ.,

OF

RACINE, WISCONSIN.

IN venturing to dedicate these lines to you, I cannot estimate with what degree of feeling they will be measured by yourself, nor how a general public will sit in judgment over my audacity, leaving the quality of my work entirely out of the case. Still, as I hope you will reflect kindly upon the motive, I trust the world will forgive me for placing on my first patent so good and reliable a trademark. I know it is but an old thing put forth with new trimmings—and even these are wanting in finish,—yet what there may be in fitness will go to the wardrobe of the mind's noblest issue. Not forgetting my obligations, nor expecting that they ever can be paid, I beg leave to remain,

Yours truly,

CARL ROBERT ZACHE.

INTRODUCTORY.

THE story of Hero and Leander, as told in Greek mythology, needs scarcely be related here. Merely as a nail to hang the thread upon, let it be said that they saw each other at a festival of Venus in Sestos, where the maiden served at the altars of that goddess. Leander, of Abydos in Mysia, nightly swam across the Hellespont to meet his mistress, her relatives and position forbidding a union between the two. One tempestuous night he was drowned, and when, in the morning, Hero beheld the lifeless form of her lover, she threw herself into the sea.

HERO AND LEANDER.

As two great fires, burning to unite,

    Consume their courses with high-leaping flames,

Being now pale, now red, now dark, now white,

    Till hot embraces end their mutual aims ;

        So burned both Hero's and Leander's mood,

        So were both quenched, so starved with lack

            of food !

For fires have light from what they do destroy,

    And lovers from what they reject with scorn ;

Both scorch in contact, where they would but toy,

    On meeting both are suddenly forlorn ;

        The fires die, having no more to eat,—

        These lovers perish, being without retreat !

But see them first, the one look at the other,

　Then gaze aside, then look just twice as long ;

Each like a bird who has escaped its mother,

　To woo a mate without its mother's song.

　　They speak a language with their moving eyes,

　　Whose copious meaning more than words im-

　　　plies.

And after thus conversing for a time,

　The while their veins distil a tell-tale hue,

Which deeper shadows in their pantomime

　Could not gainsay, did they deny it true—

　　Leander seeks the altar where she prays

　　To have her hear what with his mouth he says.

"O look," begins he (strange prayer to Love's

　　　Queen),

　" My voice goes bankrupt in redeeming thought ;

Words piled on words, or scene succeeding scene,

　Could not release my meaning as they ought :

And if they could, my late attesting eyes
Would prove it faulty and my thoughts
  unwise.

The zephyr to sweet flowers sighs and sings,
 The wooing river murmurs as it flows ;
non great heat or inclination wings
 Their self-same efforts, till a whirlwind blows,
   Until a torrent roars and leaps along ;
   The world's fair orchestra now playing wrong !

Say not the lowland stream flows deep and wide
 Upon the hollow bosom of the dale ;
ay not the gentle Zephyrus does glide
 Against the green leaves and the laboring sail :
   But say, these elements make out to please,
   When steady nature does direct with ease.

O what shall time my poor heart's dissonance,
Wherein love's proceeds aggregate a moan ;

And who has guarded its proud arrogance,

    That none should ever have who did not loan ?

      What made me say, ' before I go invest

      I 'll see my love safe at high interest ? '

" For, unadvised, I 've looked but at the gain,

    And signed my heart's sole heritage away.

But the rich debtor, who, if she refrain

    To grant me tribute, will herself dismay,

      In that her own heart's wealth have no return,

      Which, left with me, she would with my love

        spurn !

" Yet happy me, no no she 'll ever say !

    And if she say no she will breathe a lie

Whose legal tender vain would be love's pay,

    Or truth's endorsed and fiat currency ;

      And if 't was true, rather than doubt her ruth,

      I 'd say that lies were true, that false were

        truth.

" And should she then pretend that she did love me,

 To prove her hate and that love's course was run,

Such sweet dissembling would shine bright above me,

 Being reflection from so great a sun,

  That I would say, ' 't is light, 't is light and

   bright ! '

  And swear, ' 't is warm ! ' if it were cold and

   night.

" This would I swear, and more, and double that ;

 And so convince myself against myself,

My love would be the judge where reason sat,

 And calculation turn upon itself.

  Glut would seem hollow, wantons continent,

  Half what is whole, bad what is excellent.

" Which straightway would induce a gossips' cry

 Of my brain's muddle and their own good sense,

How my poor judgment might feed heavily

 On their fair wit, to make my joy intense.

As if the void could weigh, being filled with no,

And sorrow cheer up, comforted with woe !

"See how the rose bends to the violet,

Which lends good color to the queen's green rug;

Heaven's gentle tears drop from her toilet,

And fall upon a beetle, bee, or bug

That, scared, flies hence to find the little
flower,

Where it does sit, wet by the summer shower.

"Now may the sun send to the royal scene

His fiery minions, the o'er-gilded rays ;

Blue heaven may smile, the breeze may rock the
queen,

And all ha' enough to drink for many days,

Where they would thirst, and blight, without
such showers,

The brief existence of small life and flowers.

"Thus, too, O Venus," closed the speaking youth,
   As if his words still lacked of their intent,
"Incline your godly grace to her, forsooth,
   Who is your temple's modest ornament:
      Who pleads your beauty's cause so well below,
      And whose sweet presence makes your king-
         dom grow."

With this Leander closed his thought's flood-gate,
   And dammèd up love's freshet in his brain.
He must now home, and can no longer wait,
   Where he would never leave, could he remain;
      He sees Hero's white color change to red,
      And thinks it answers all that he has said.

But she is undone, fearful, and inflamed,
   Being now cold, now hot—now hot, now cold;
She clasps her cheeks, and is of them ashamed
   For so betraying her as she is told.

She would compel her hot blood not to flow,

And of a heart refractious learns to know.

Which, though it marshal at her will's command

The scarlet forces to its citadel,

Is swift to send them on desire's demand,

That is most sweet when it does most rebel :

That says enjoy, when prudence says refrain,

That leads to ruin when good caution 's slain.

And now she trembles like the tender fawn

That meets the hunter in the woodland shade,

Or like the young dove, in the early dawn,

That spies the eagle o'er the distant glade ;

She hides her face, though he is gone away,

And bates her breath to hear what next he 'll

say.

She knew of love as being sweet and strong,

But knew not love that precludes all dissem-

bling ;

She dreamt of love, of music, and of song,
　But not of passion, fear, distrust, and trembling ;
　　She swears she hates him when she is most hot,
　　And then repeats his say since he can not.

If subtle practices could love outdo,
　Sweet love would be outdone at every turn ;
But love 's away while Hermes hunts a shoe—
　And Mercury still hunts at love's return !
　　When he is done, swift light has scarce pro-
　　　gressed,
　　Thought 's gone a mile from one in thought
　　　distressed.

And thus it is that love love's hangman is,
　An executioner where he did crown ;
His warrant is the vow, his seal the kiss,
　Fidelity his sheriff, death his frown !
　　The world is judge—and he is yet to be
　　That moves the cold world to a mild decree !

'T is said that love is to man's soul loadstone,
  Which he ignores when presumes control
Of its direction, in his youth's hot zone,
    Through temp'rate climes, to life's slow turning
        pole :
      The compass guides the lab'ring ship at sea,
      But rests awhile when ships in harbor be.

If so be love, true love is like two stars
  Whose brilliant orbs do shine upon each other ;
They course the heavens in their golden cars,
    Apollo here, and here Apollo's brother :
      Destruction can't leave one but must take both
      And so must true love die upon its oath.

The more that Hero would forget Leander,
  The more she thinks, were he within my reach !
The more she 'd sleep, the more her thoughts me-
        ander
  On the broad meaning of his level speech.

Her heart's great river, rushing from its source,
Scarce feeds the rank growth in its tortuous
course.

Another day has almost come when sleep
Kisses away her tears and fans her head.
Blushing Aurora takes an envious peep
As Morpheus mounts her mortal rival's bed—
Then fades away. Nor does she long to stay
When often thus she must announce the day !

" Why is her chamber lit night after night ? "
Queries Leander on the other shore ;
" Wherefore these vigils ? Surely I was right,
And if right rudely pains, it heals the sore ;
Her gentle heart's wound healed, she now in-
clines
For my reception, and with waiting pines !

" Nay, it is so. Her heart's deep-harrowed field
Proved far too fertile for what love had sown.

Why is spring late, where winter's snow must yield ?
  Come, Zephyrus and Flora is your own ! "
    And while he spoke he waded in the main,
    And swam for Europe's shore from Asia's plain.

If ever oceans bouyed a better freight
  Than young Leander, 't was not human kind ;
If stronger arms propelled a heavier weight,
  The greater bulk needs had a coarser rind.
    An endless ripple, like a maiden's band,
    Surrounds his throat and stretches for the
      strand.

His step is slow, his breathing quick, in Thrace ;
  But soon slow breathing quickens his slow walk.
The light is near, and near the light a face
  Whose eyes, he knows, though not its mouth, did
    talk.
    Before he scales the rocks he prays to Jove
    That his reward may be the maiden's love.

And waking, Hero, called upon to hear,

  Outreasons hesitation readily ;

Saying : " Alas, that what I love is near,

  What I despise is tendered steadily.

    What now I take is mine ! " and then she bade

    Leander to ascend the last steep grade.

Look, how two panthers—smooth, swift, fierce, and

    black—

  Engage each other on the mountain side ;

Where the pale moon unveils a fav'ring crack,

  Through which the warm wind breathes, loth to

    abide.

    The night's soft shadows glide, the silence

    throbs,

    The future flirts with time, the old past sobs.

Like chiselled darkness through the haze they move,

  His eyes two coals, her two great embers eyes ;

His breath hot steam, her lungs' steam breath does

    prove ;

  His neck, stretched long (with hers, forsooth,

    likewise),

    Joins a deep chest, thin flanks, strong legs,

      sharp claws,

    To a round head, short ears, white teeth, strong

      jaws.

Eager to prove his love, he courts the rocks,

  Drawing his soft sides o'er the senseless stone ;

Thus may I please (he means), and thus may I (she

    mocks) ;

  Behold my strength (he leaps), she shows her

    own ;

    He grows impatient, but she still is slow,

    Cooling her stronger heat with his great glow.

Whereat the foam does quiver on his lips

  Which open at the poor nerves' discontent,

Whose lavish force the muscles' strength so clips,

    That to new efforts no reserve is sent.

        So must a galley with its slaves capsize

        That beats the rough sea for a captious prize.

Prone on the earth the poor wretch now reposes,

    While she in weak defiance curves her back.

Soon he his love, and she her teeth discloses,

    Than better quality do neither lack.

        Her teeth cloak love, his strong love teeth and

            pain,

        The which both fear to swap with fleeting gain.

As heaven's brilliant huntress, in her chase,

    Behind the cover of some cloud-bush darts,

Leaps the black male the female to embrace—

    Those two join well whom love's defiance parts :

        Poor, piteous love, in arbors so agile,

        In armor clumsy, may now rest awhile.

What lover would not enter when his lady

　　Opens her chamber on a summer's night ?

Who sweats that scorns to lie where it is shady ?

　　Who thirsts that runs from water at its sight ?

　　　Who, being poor, would take not proffered

　　　　treasures ?

　　　Who, sick, refuse health, strength, long life, and

　　　　pleasures ?

Look, love is sick and poor, and thirsts, and sweats,

　　Until it have what is beyond its keeping ;

To madman's visage it joins tyrants' threats,

　　To soft angelic features mantled weeping ;

　　　Thwarted it rages, in success it smiles,

　　　Fair promises it trusts, sense it beguiles.

It is a storm upon the sea of life,

　　Affection's trade-wind, blowing round good hope !

The undeceived sail with its due course rife,

　　Others defy it, perish, or elope ;

On oath their phantoms still surmount time's

    waves,

To goad strong fools and terrify weak knaves.

Now is the trader safe on India's shore,

    And loads of pleasures deep down into cares ;

Exultingly he counts his goods—wants more,

    Then apprehends a loss of all his wares ;

        To quell his fear, he thinks of that rich gain

        Which his contentment holds beyond the main.

O how is love so certain in its prime

    Of joys to volunteer against life's woes !

How fares its army, to the march of time,

    On meeting envy, who does smile her noes !

        Did love but think—but no, better have love

        unwise

        Than with it knowing blacken all the skies.

Too apt is love to boast of what it lacks,

    Thinking its wants supplied when it needs naught ;

Too late it gathers strength to meet attacks,

    Too soon it is out-generaled and caught

        It hears a troth and says, dead is all craft,

        Deceit a myth, then throws away its shaft.

Th' self-wounded love-god, to obtain a mate,

    Agreed to handicap the hypogriph ;

His wings were clipped, and who could rise in state,

    Toiled against odds o'er mountain, plain, and

        cliff—

        Ah, true love never ran a race so close,

        Than when he spurred the youth of Abydos !

His body's strength his father's life reports,

    His fertile mind his gentle mother's care,

His sight his tongue in idleness supports,

    (Who profits not with such a pensioner ?)

        The beauteous picture in this well-wrought

        frame,

        Hangs in suspense, a prize to Sesto's fame !

Who now could see them nothing else would see,
  For nothing else such harmony implies.
Who now would hear them nothing loud could flee,
  For all is silent, all is hushed ; no cries,
    No shrill discord, no grating sound, no shriek,
    Mars the melodious meeting on this peak.

" O sweetest eyes," he sues, " why shade your light ?
  Vouchsafe my own e'en but a single ray
And day shall come where morning wars with night,
  Though all the heavens be hung in black dismay ;
    For that shall melt like summer-clouds of rain,
    In which your love-light shall have seven-fold
      gain !

" Can I boast conquest, where I do not sway
  Save as a vassal on my queen's estate ?
Then is my love sweet but for to betray,
  And my sweet love may well bar her heart's gate
    Now I am near ; for so the treacherous mind
    To please their vanity while being kind.

" Nor trust the coinage of my pleasing speech,

   Whose value weight alone may indicate ;

But say he lies whose love attempts to teach,

   He loves that wearies lab'ring o'er a slate !

      Then add one word of all you have in store,

      Or look that word, and I will ask no more ! "

And with his overture's key-note refrain

   She does applaud him from her soul's look-out,

She tenders every flow'r in her domain

   A thousand times to drive away his doubt !

      And he with silence still on her imposes

      That he may kiss the lilies and red roses !

" To say but little to acquit so much

   Limits," she 'gins, " my dues as your heart's wit-

      ness ;

Whereas my love's greed would not limit such,

   But all in love still nourish your doubt's fitness

To still prolong the trial of your eye,

That I might still be called to testify !

" To tell you truly yes when I look no,

To say I lie when I do claim you wrong ;

To chide myself, and kiss you so, and so,

When I refuse your kisses short or long ;

To hug you dearly when I grudge my charms,

And perish nearly distant from your arms !

" Where are the words that inkle at my meaning,

Where is their sum, the time for my expression ?

And where am I, so strong, (strange sight,) found

leaning,

That should, not well, avoid the least compression ?

If so the body answers my heart's strain,

Judge not the words that do attend the brain.

" But rather think them doves, yourself a-hunting,

I am the fairy awkward with the reins,

With your wit's dart you shoot my poor wit's stunt-
  ing,
 And my shell coach you string for gentle strains ;
  Which, being done, I can in silence sit
  Where with much talk I am not fit a bit.

'' But fear I have, my father's slumb'ring hate
 May wake upon the music of this news,
A rank discord to our hearts' concert's state
 That has no second audience to lose ;
  But, having once displeased, the patrons go,
  And all engagements end with such a no

" Though love's small manager still bend his bow ! "
 "Now verily," he warns, "your thoughts must
  change
Or love's warm charge will freeze on logic's snow.
 A shallow mouth does shipwrecked hopes es-
  trange,
  Griefs, being harbored, sink and so abide
  Till o'er life's bar they do with sure death tide.

" Fools feast upon the salt at reason's spread,

   When dainties tempt the palate of their praise ;

None scorn the wine for water and for bread

   (What pleasure serves for soberness) always.

      Were a great river straight the source would

      weep

    Seeing the outlet in far ocean's deep.

" Each curve 's a hope, each bend an expectation,

   Nor yet forlorn until the very last.

A friendly bid receives an inundation,

   The uninviting rocks are quickly passed ;

     The tributary meets a kind embrace,

     And both now whisper, flowing face to face ! "

" I listen to the waters," she replies,

   " Whose smooth performance limns th' receding

      shore,

That yields, all vanity, at such a price,

   And blossoms red and white all o'er and o'er.

No maid, wooed well, but what vies with good

    grace,

Printing her heart's stamp on her open face.

" A summer's heat follows the hast'ning spring,

    When the parched earth implores the stream to

        lave it ;

There to sustain where it caused every thing :

    But lo, the river heeds not now to save it ;

        Askance it glides, seeking the woodland cover ;

        A shallow, narrow, and a lukewarm lover !

" At heaven's commanding frown comes plenteous

    rain,

    Whose myriad kisses swell the jealous stream

To overflow and make his bed amain

    Where resting rain-drops cause the flow'rs to

        dream.

    A man's love dies for what no one admires :

    That being wished for kindles his desires.

" The river's downward course becomes a flood,

   Straight on the surface, crooked on the heath ;

Th' uprooted pine, sharp-pointed, drags through mud

   And then is fixed insidious underneath !

     Truth may become a snag in dirty lies,

     And sink from sight a mansion in the skies.

" Behold the stains of licensed jealousy,

   (Most soiling to the lily's purity),

A mortgage made to spite by fallacy,

   Wherewith to foreclose love's futurity.

     That happiness fail of maturity,

     The envious hint at vile obscurity."

This said she breaks from his environment

   In apprehension of her love's starvation,

Within the ramparts of such armament,

   Should naught prevent her waste and devastation.

     Like a deserter who does love his life

     She leaves the fort, fearing relentless strife.

" Farewell," she says.   He asks her : " why good-
      bye ? "
Her tongue 's too heavy to disclose her head.
Far seems the window whither she does hie,
   Long the few seconds, her sad heart of lead.
      The moon's stray beams seem cold, her disk of
        light
      A mile-stone in the realm of death and night.

Look, when the lily, overcome by rain,
   Droops her pale head, the sun's relief is nigh ;
Or when the palm-tree's crown bends to the plain,
   The night-wind heralds comfort with a sigh !
      The tulip longs for shade, for warmth the aster,
      And the great sun averts from both disaster.

As when the bud opens the second morn,
   That through one night has mourned the death
      of day,
So this sweet maid is not so all-forlorn
   That Lean's step could heighten her dismay.

Nay, she is but a blooming flow'r, at best,
That chid the sun when he was in the west.

His touch and sight comfort poor Hero's sorrow,
  As when the stag comes to defend the hind.
As when the red clouds tell of fair to-morrow
  So her to-day is by his red cheeks lin'd ;
    Her girdle his strong arms—his necklace hers ;
    Both now enjoy what poets dream in verse.

Her eyes, he tells her, are to his an ocean
  That rests at night upon a starry floor ;
His heart, wrecked on the billows of emotion,
  Finds a sweet end, believing death heaven's door.
    She tells him if her eyes are a great sea,
    He sees himself, and dies himself to see.

" 'T was wrong [he then] what I described before !
  The rising tide is in my arms' deep bay ;
A flood of ripples kiss the curving shore,
  While lower down the heaving billows play."

She asks : "What, if the tide should ebb?"

He says :

" Tide, love, and hope around a circle race.

" The onward wave does come again this way,

Red lips begin where need enjoined repairs ;

Eyes but repeat what they looked yesterday,

And tongues reiterate old joys and cares.

Pleasure ceases now, for never at an end

'T is strained of sweetness till the bulk offend."

" O then this love," she says, " is not of pleasure,

But something else, if else can never tire.

And if all tires, love then is such a treasure,

That he who steals from love takes his own hire ;

Ill-gotten wealth is very soon destroyed,

Or, still increasèd, nevermore enjoyed.

" The silly thief who purloins dues from life,

Is he not punished with enforced decay ?

An ill-used whetstone dulls the sharpest knife,

    Though dull knives' ease take edges from a tray.

      Shall we not manage what we have in mind,

      That it may profit where we now must grind ? "

And he is pleased to have her so unsheath,

    And will surrender to the well-made thrust ;

And she, the victor, claims a myrtle wreath,

    And will consign her weapon now to rust ;

      Needing no more for petty conquest's sake,

      What captured him who furrowed Helle's

      lake.

O if such talk could but arrest swift time,

    Or stay sure death, both time and death would

      cease !

One word or two might warm a wintry clime,

    Ten thousand words prolong the summer's lease !

      But that it fails of this these lovers see,

      As ruddy morning causes night to flee.

Then both unlock, and he prepares to go.

Come such necessity with its farewell !

Efforts say yes, embraces answer no,

Kisses renew, if dull words break the spell :

The longest kiss leads but a mighty train,

When that is gone the long kiss comes again !

What more than nurse can any gard'ner do ;

What more Leander to raise true affection ?

Night after night he bids sweet sleep adieu,

And welcomes toil to make hers all perfection !

O why should his success the fates provoke

To make her ivy-love kill his love's oak ?

What is a year to never-waking sleep ?

What is a day to heaven-dreaming love ?

What is a tear to those who always weep ?

What is a home to those who ever move ?

What is a bite to the starved epicure,

Beauty to lust, hope to the young and pure ?

With each draught tipplers drink desire for more,

  Each night augments this love-intoxication.

Repeated strife still keeps the old wounds sore—

  Is not the sweetest peace of short duration?

    Who can enjoy what by long use displeases;

    Who knows health's value knowing not diseases?

A month is gone (time's palate craves such honey),

  Her heart's retort distils the same sweet sight.

His bullion thought he coins in bright new money,

  Her purse of joy is heavy with delight!

    Though he is drunk from her strong spirit's still,

    He pays a dear price for another fill.

"O see," she pleads, "the season seems to tarry,

  For still the Philomel enjoys night's glory.

A thousand crickets say 'we-we' (we marry),

  Will you not promise to repeat that story

    To-morrow night?   I'll pray for restful seas,

    I'll pray our queen the ocean's god to please!

"And as you wish, I shall prepare to go ; —
  Make this your troth, for it is my condition.
I 've oft applied—you never answered no ; —
  Shall this last tax conjure a black sedition ?
    Hold, do not chide, love ! Neither does the
      moon
    When asked why sometimes she appears at
      noon.

" You 'll come, for sure, to end a little May
  For warmer sunshine and a growing June.
Good-night to you—good-morning to the day !
  Love's ended feast divorces dish and spoon ;
    The tiny god is full, and to his joy
    Th' oft-tested metal proves without alloy.

" What matters then the form of ownership ?
  Love is a thief, I cannot well restrain him.
The canny burglar holds me in his grip ;
  No dungeon now can possibly contain him !

A hope is left me though : That from afar

  His depredations force one heart ajar."

Whereby she means her sire's, whose stubborn will

  Discounts the rose by thought of crimson paint.

He long ago perceived his daughter ill,

  Though not the loved cause of her sad complaint ;

    And as he sleeps secure she 's wide-awake,

    Praying for Lean, who is in the lake.

Then as the gray-and-silver-liveried east

  Admits the swelled face of the redolent sun,

Tired Leander with his blood appeased,

  Joins to the wet road the more solid one.

    He walks apace, all shivering, pinched, and blue,

    An incorporate rebellion overdue.

"What outcast I, that nightly prowls with fear

  (So war in civil strife his legion thought) ;

What churl, what clown, what body out of gear,

  What simple mind, what slave unsold or bought ?

No danger fear I, fearing this one danger,

That proud dislikes may thwart a prouder

    stranger.

"Is my strong purpose strained from folly's curd,

  Or does pale wisdom's milk buoy up such bravery?

If peril courted makes the deed absurd,

  Why valor then in me is selfish knavery;

    Whereon my friends of busy tongue and eye

    Shall wait with sport and salient mockery.

"Then this black sea-throat shall be yet discounted,

  And tortured me shall enter hells of pain!

More hideous shapes — by strength to be sur-

    mounted—

  Than in the gulf, shall float about my brain:

    Nor shall they sink from sight on sleep's calm

    shore,

    But in the bog of dreams suck at my sore.

" If love be blind it should be sharp of hearing—
    Well, so it is, if its fair mistress sigh.
Fondly it dares, and daring is endearing ;
    Naught dives so deep nor soars so very high.
        No virtue is so staid, no fault so wild,
        That could not well pay tribute to this child.

" Now am I made ashamed in consciousness
    For fighting it with such a sore lament ;
I deck my favors with my griefs' undress,
    That gain may lessen here, here loss augment.
        Soon shall I say : O what a rogue am I
        To rail at heaven since it is so high !

" And never think this sky upon my back,
    And never fear its all-disastrous fall ;
And never know my safety from attack,
    And never feel the danger I forestall
        Under this load, which love made seem so light
        With the sweet vision of an angel's sight."

What else he thinks—who lives can half portray it ?
   Or, partly told, what patience there to hear ?
The sun from oceans drinks, yet men essay it
   As sucking from the fen and hidden wier !
      Men think wits foolish that enjoy small things,
      Until at sea with these their natural kings.

His chilled imagination southward goes,
   Like northern air that holds but little vapor ;
Or arctic ice, or stiff-necked buffaloes
   (That 's sure to melt, or which begin to caper).
      Such is the progress made that by the night
      His pole of reason loses its affright,

Or, more, becomes possessed of fascination,
   As winter to the toiler in June's sun ;
Who swears such heat is dire abomination,
   Recalls the snow, the fresh air, and the fun ;
      Thinks of his comfort at the fire, while now
      He cools the earth with water from his brow.

Leander measures shadows like young grain,

    Upon whose ripeness he may realize ;

And at the harvest would of toil complain,

    As rich ones whom more gold does tantalize.

        Sometimes they set their teeth, and so does he,

        Sometimes they fail—he says that shall not be.

Poor boy, he sweats.   There is a dead calm o'er him,

    And roundabout the twilight hangs like lead.

What he now sees is her red torch before him,—

    He 'd see no more were ten eyes in his head ;

        And if he did, his love-lost brain, in rage,

        Would cry the curtain o'er each optic's stage.

The gull's shrill cry, the surf's dull, hollow peal,

    In vain besiege the office of his ear.

Soon round his thighs the sea's low swell does deal,

    And now he yields his weight to disappear.

        His head buoys up, he turns upon his side,

        That his broad chest may better plow the tide.

Night's darkness veils him. Black, tempestuous
      night
Seems summoned to prevent the death of day,
Whose heavenly orb, like to the Cyclop's sight,
    Might cease, being stabbed in this poor lad's
       affray :
      Who is now rocked by death to be at rest,
      Though starved for life that flows from nature's
       breast.

Look, how the petty tyrant of one hour
    Inflicts the measure of his murderous brain ;
Or how the slave treats others in his power,
    Knowing that soon he mayhap share their pain :
      Even so this storm, thus suddenly released,
      Rides on the sea's smooth back from west to
       east.

First quivers the poor steed at flat-fall'n gusts,
    That mark the spurring rider's ugly will.

Then, trembling, heaves, as thrusts do follow
   thrusts,
 Until each round pore foams, being used so ill.
  By fury lashed, the patient anger slow,
  And even wroth they 're quiet well below.

Yet woe to those that trusted their support
 In an old bottom of some dead wit's make.
He 's soon disposed of who, without resort,
 Steals to be topmost when the dull awake.
  And such a luckless, self-reliant thief
  Is this Leander's strength, now come to grief.

Its sly accomplice—Thracian Hero's beauty—
 Appears inclined to favor black-veiled Nox,
Even as men love toil, when care and duty,
 Debarring sorrow, solve the paradox.
  But beauty has no will—like strength it dies
  If what can save is far, or, near, soon flies.

It cannot even weather brief suspense,
 Becoming homely in one hour of fright.
Fool that it is, it waits on giddy sense,
 Seeking in manners loud its chief delight :
  And when demurely clad it seems to cry,
  O see how fair and lovable am I !

First coveted in health, last in disease,
 It is the mistress of endangered pride.
Oh, Hero is not well in this stiff breeze ;
 She thinks not of her face, her form, her side,
  Her ruby lips, 'neath which her teeth parade,
  Her eyes' clear lustre or their lashes' shade.

She has ten fevers, all combined in one,
 And ten times ten, t' fire her imagination.
Each thundering breaker causes her to run,
 Each lull to stop and hope his preservation ;
  To list for every sound, and noise, and cry,
  And then to swear : " He is too good to die !

" I am but selfish to invent this scare,

　　Which stamps him rash who certainly is wise,

As if he needs for me must do and dare !—

　　When oaths of love are wrong one may revise !

　　　But did he, did he ? Was he warned in time ?"

　　　This she repeats to make an endless rhyme.

Who has not watched the tigress in her cage,

　　When boundless freedom beckoned through the

　　　　bars ;

Look, how her love dispels her sullen rage,

　　And one desire enacts an eager farce ;

　　　From end to end she whisks without repose,

　　　Still trying all the narrows with her nose.

Behind the bars she seems a purblind beast,

　　Decrepit, weak, and not without her grievance ;

Pity is moved, the sense of wrong increased :

　　The sense of wrong holds self-love in obeisance ;

The sympathies enlist to fight the reason,
As thaws the winter in the coldest season.

But pity, conscience, and compassion fly,
And fear, surprise, and admiration enter,
When feline hunger marks the young lamb's cry,
And she the prison-grate that does prevent her.
Lo, in the dungeon night Hero 's confined,
Famished for love, whereof before she dined !

Where smitten Oceanus wrought the stone
That now adòrns usurper Neptune's throat,
This love-lorn woman ventures all alone :
Self-castigation does her peace promote ;
The staggering breaker and the rugged path
Are antidotes to stay her conscience' wrath.

Since all her faculties serve but on hearing,
Making that sense a novice with new power,

She often harks—her every part appearing
  With as much life as marble would allow her.
    Her lungs cease to expand, her heart does stop,
    While perspiration yields drop after drop.

At last she seats herself, all tired with pacing,
  And steeps her anguish in the balm of tears ;
Which boon relieves the strain with kind solacing,
  Undoes remorse, and sways the maddening fears.
    The crystal fountains that showed heaven by
      day
    Submit their flow night's sorrow to allay.

" Oh, if he is no more [thus she divines],
  A world is dead whereof but I remain ;
Bright hope for me no longer warmly shines,
  But spreads a pallor o'er a cold domain,
    Where my killed love-thoughts, like the sweet-
      est flow'rs,
    Through one short cycle did beguile the hours !

" If he is dead, all else shall die with weeping ;

   If he is dead, no more shall come to life.

His death and chaos shall be in good keeping ;

   His death with new creation be in strife :

     The silent void, through all eternity,

     Shall be the tomb for him who so did die !

" But if he lives ! " (O happy germ of thought

   To fall upon such rich imagination !)

" Then with his life new heavens shall be bought,

   And every shade be ransomed to salvation !

     He, living, shall be truth's own victory,

     Falsehood's despair, and faith's felicity ! "

And then she paints the canvas of her brain

   With countless scenes of future happiness,

From which her love shall wipe away each stain

   That memory of trials may impress.

     Her execution she commends with cause,

     And joyfully predicts the world's applause

Until a heavy doze unstrings anxiety,—

    Whereon her being played accompaniment,—

And clears thought's stage of overdone variety,

    (What consciousness does such relief lament?)

        Ah, if the sinner could buy dreamless sleep,

        Sin's harvest would have come, and lust would

           reap.

Shame would be dead where it is now rebelling,

    And fear a myth where now it is a giant;

Of just rewards quaint legends would be telling,

    A thousand joys of every act defiant:

        No passion could be conquered, for desire,

        Forever keen, forever would strike fire.

Where now the battle rages peace would reign;

    Where fevers follow health would be the leader;

Where snow falls early now frosts would abstain;

    Where all is now a book 't would be the reader;

Where levies now deplete, 't would gain in
    kind,
And all would flourish in the sinner's mind,

Which is so full of danger and confusion,
    Of apprehension, labor, and distrust,
When ill-timed sleep effects a sly intrusion,
    Beguiles the senses to forsake their trust,
        Prompts fancy, and adorns imagination
        For making sport of space and calculation.

Yet softly treading time has more than cunning
    When woman's love falls short in expiation,
And retribution does excel in dunning
    When it applies before her own donation ;
        She poises on a pivot, swings from heaven,
        To each disturbance she replies with seven.

To her regrets Hero has made such answer,
    And, self-convicted, wrought the punishment,

That not this night shall cruel conscience lance her,

  Or strain her hold upon the firmament :

    Lo, even where she sits the rocks begin

    To yield her comfort ; and with her white skin

The ravished night brings forth a hybrid haze,

  As if the stars did wed thin clouds a bit ;

To be inhaled by her the cold wind stays

  (No howling wolf e'er died in such a pit).

    Her bosom gently heaves, which to the sea

    Disputes what is, suggests what ought to be.

Now it is still and morning, and she wakes,

  For in a battle silence does alarm.

The furious storm has ceased to churn for flakes,

  And every billow seems a smooth white arm,

    The which some sea-nymph did protrude with

      grace,

    Courting a loved man's kiss and sweet embrace.

At first the outlines her memory's state

    Appear too indistinct for recollection :

She is but dreaming, and the hour is late ;

    There is, she thinks, from bad dreams no pro-

        tection.

        Suddenly she starts, as if some breaking light

        Conquered a mist that veilèd her clear sight.

Then all at once, as lagging fire, fanned,

    Creeps through dark coals, her eyes begin to

        glisten ;

Her purple cheeks deny that blood is scant,

    Wherefore the past to th' brain so fed does listen ;

        Answering quickly with each fright and hope

        That stabbed her joy or did with fear elope.

From her unwonted seat she quickly rises—

    Pains go for naught amid a fear for life.

No pent-up king reflects on bad advises,

    Or sends a needed force to lesser strife.

Hero is ruled by love—that love commands,

Nor will it hear the bleeding feet and hands.

Where the bold earth rounds toward heaven she

    scrambles,

  Still counting over possibilities.

Her own love and devotion she preambles

  In her distress ; with his abilities

    She builds the resolutions of her heart,

    That he must live whose life does life impart.

It seems so grand, the future she has made,

  That critic death, though he condemn, might pity,

And stay his blow for an unwilling shade

  That loathes dark Pluto and his shapeless city.

    " Alas," she says, " alas, good death, forbear !

    Or, if already cut, engraft him there !

" Between these arms his lifeless form shall quicken ;

  Upon these lips his own begin to glow ;

With this upheaving breast his chest shall thicken,
  His eyes shall ope, his strength begin to grow !
    For he has sworn that dead within these arms
    He 'd live again — again he 'd love these
      charms ! "

Thus speaking she has gained the steep ascent
  From which her spirit shall begin its flight.
Alas, poor bird, why is it not content
  When from its nest it sees its loved mate's plight ;
    But 'gins to cry, as he that brought sweet store,
    With too much caught succumbs and is no more ?

Lo, in this solemn hour of last resort,
  Wherein her eyes do turn death's evidence,
And every fibre calls for strong support,
  She bows to fate, accepts the consequence ;
    Looks on the earth, her home ; on heaven, so
      fair ;
    Then deeply breathes the vigorous morning air.

Look, love's a tree and grief a parasite

   Whose stem the woodman first of all does sever.

Love lives when grief is dead—yet is contrite ;

   Grief crooked grows, love not ; grief bends, love

      never.

      Grief seconds grinning hatred, which ascends

      To tear the homes of heaven-seeking friends.

O love's presumption to o'ertop the clouds

   Is ever born anew and ever dying !

Now crowned with roses, and now wrapped in

      shrouds,

   Now bathed in sunshine, now in darkness lying,

      It first says things are better which are worse,

      And lastly that this life is but a curse.

Like some poor artist, doomed to starvation,

   That still must paint, or chisel love from stone,

Hero does make this humble explanation

   (The human heart shall hear, though she 's alone):

"Since all my life floats dead upon the main,
  I cannot kill myself or die again ;

"But will I bear sweet company unto him,
  And lead my funeral to his large tomb.
Already stars grow dim, having passed to view him ;
  Now sun go slow lest you may share their doom ;
    Or, if you cannot curb your daily speed,
    Look but on me who caused this dark misdeed—

"This murder foul, this crime, this execution—
  O it shall taint forever nature's name ;
Forever men shall think of this pollution,
  This rape of beauty, and this ocean's shame !
    Yea, rising sun, look presently and see
    A small atonement in inanimate me !

"Now I 'll divest my soul of memories dear—
  Old garments they, yet O how fair when new !
Childhood is faded, save where it was near ;

My first ambition's crown. itself withdrew

    When love came by and beckoned with this
        wreath

    Whose golden band is torn with him beneath.

" Methinks a poet, whose slow-forgèd rhyme

    Has conquering bravery's polished armor proved,

Would scarce bewail its loss in that far time

    When men shall suffer slavery unmoved :

      So, too, the author of my life may say :

      ' 'T is well she 's dead, since love has passed
        away.'

" For true love perished with my true love's breath-
        ing,

    Which opened beauteous portals to the air,

Warming the bathers, where hot springs were seeth-
        ing ;

    From east, west, north, and south—from every-
        where

Æolian patients sought my true love's breast,

Whose currents, stopped, swell those of my un-

rest.

" He often held this hand—come hither, hand,

And be the proxy in a last sweet kiss !

O fie, that you can't speak at my command,

For if you could you 'd say : ' One is amiss,

Two will not do, ten thousand won't suffice,—

An endless kiss shall be my paradise ! '

" Then you would say, perhaps, that I do wrong

To double nature's loss in him in me,

And urge the earth would gain if I 'd live long—

No, no ; 't is better that you silent be.

My life's broad desert is so hot and dreary

That an oasis would but make me weary.

" Be well content ; you also ; likewise you.

In a head-conquered state the limbs are slaves.

You 've given good support, you will be true—

I would not call vain cowards to their graves !

    The end is there ; it would be just as near

    If endless life were chased by endless fear ! "

More she can't say, swift action does prevent her,

    As braves their chief, when he would urge them

        still.

Her simple words' result may well content her,

    That send her body headlong from the hill ;

        At whose steep base she renders up her soul,

        While pitying waves conduct her to the goal.

There, in the lake ; look, what a strange love-

        marriage !

The air is hushed ; the waters crowd to see !

Time is amazed at its own fond miscarriage ;

    The surf peals forth a wond'ring melody !

        The white-robed sun comes forth with meas-

        ured pace :

        "'T is done, 't is done," all listening nature

        says !

See, see, O see what never yet was seen :

Departed lovers seek their bridal bed !

They sleep beneath a canopy of green ;

They would not wake if it were colored red.

By chance her corpse does fall across his own,

And all is still to hear the love-god moan !

www.ingramcontent.com/pod-product-compliance
Lightning Source LLC
Chambersburg PA
CBHW021528090426
42739CB00007B/830